Don't Forget: You're Still Alive

Caring for the Brain and Memory as We Age

KIMBERLY MITCHELL

Archway Publishing books may be ordered through booksellers or by contacting:

Archway Publishing
1663 Liberty Drive
Bloomington, IN 47403
www.archwaypublishing.com
844-669-3957

ISBN: 978-1-6657-3346-5 (sc)
ISBN: 978-1-6657-3347-2 (e)

Library of Congress Control Number: 2022921110

Print information available on the last page.

Archway Publishing rev. date: 12/12/2022

Dedicated to my Aunt Judy.
ALL glory and honor to God.

CONTENTS

FOREWORD

As I write about Kimberly Mitchell, a woman I've been the closest kind of friend with for 20 years, I know, reader, that you probably won't believe what I tell you. Then why would I waste my very valuable time, as well as yours, writing a foreword that reads like a myth? I'm writing because I need you, oh blessed finder of this book, to understand the spirit from whom these writings derive.

I have never, and I mean *never*, met a person like Kimberly Mitchell. She has the most helpful, loving spirit I've ever encountered, and baby, I've traveled in this lifetime. I've met bishops, beggars, billionaires, and a gaggle of in-betweens. Mitchell, as I call her, has the kind of light that calms inner oceans and lifts seemingly insurmountable mountains. She's a unicorn. I've watched her pour love into every room she enters, whether she's cooking for somebody or tutoring another (working flawlessly at both); whether she's helping me give birth to my wonderful somebody or planting flowers for someone else or if she's writing the book your body is activated by, this beautiful, ever-so-kind, intelligent woman will bring you joy.

Kimberly Mitchell wants you to succeed. She wants you to live fully. She wants you continually blossoming, ever blooming. I thank Jehovah for Kimberly Mitchell's presence in my life and in yours. Abundant blessings on your journey, reader. Writing this sincere truth about my inspiring friend has been my honor.

Love and Light,
Dr. Jill Scott
Mother, Writer, Artist, Poet, Actress …

INTRODUCTION

I was moved to research memory and brain health when one of my close aunts began to show signs of neurological decline. She was the best cook on my paternal side, and there was nothing more special to her than family gatherings. I never saw her without a smile. I can still hear her laughing. The family began to notice some of her best recipes tasting slightly off, and she would mention forgetting small things, like one digit in a phone number she typically knew without flaw. Yes, the one or two missing ingredients, the random number disappearing from her mind, and the frequent repetition of stories or statements were all initial signs of memory loss.

Her decline was slow, but it was surely taking place. It was heart-wrenching to watch. Not only did her personal suffering take a toll on me, but watching my uncle and cousins gradually see her memories, their memories, fade away was a sort of torture. After all, our memories are the stories that make our older years so beautiful. All of our experiences, good and not so good, equal up to who we are continuously becoming. How traumatic it must be to mix up and delete the files in our mind that provide us our very essence. ***Memory loss is the ultimate pilferer, a canny swindler of oneself.*** Victims of Alzheimer's disease and dementia are left helpless and oftentimes lost. My aunt spent intentional time and energy creating a life worth remembering. These illnesses stole from her like a thief in the night. That's when I felt the need to take a rooted stance. But how?

Living on the other side of the country, away from most of my family, forced me to take action through anticipating strangers. ***The universe started revealing people and places that needed realistic information about protecting the aging mind.*** I began to research and study brain and memory health. Any and everything I could read, I read. Any studies I was privy to, I also read. Any seminars and lectures I could attend, I did. Then, out of the blue, I got a call from an agency I was independently tutoring children through to cover for another tutor. The assignment was teaching memory care at three different senior facilities for six weeks. I didn't hesitate to accept.

Just a week in, I was fully invested in becoming a healthy resource for the senior community. My peppy personality and positive outlook on life were attributes that made my audiences loosen up and listen. I felt I had my aunt in a new form. After all, I had the loving relatives of so many people in my care. Call it divine intervention, purpose, or whatever you choose; *I felt a mission was placed in front of me and I was extremely excited to meet the challenge.*

In 2014, I developed and birthed "Brain Booster Class with Kimberly." This class lasts an hour, twice a month. I teach individuals privately and in group settings at senior residences and facilities. Attendees show up with a notebook, pen, and some level of cerebral curiosity. I show up with structured, beneficial information and oodles of my bouncy, bubbly energy. Week after week, month after month, year after year, they still show up. I'm so very proud of this fact; it proves that *people are taking action to improve their brain health*.

Teaching memory care through my Brain Booster class has been one of the most rewarding ventures of my life. Selfishly, I admit I gain just as much as I give. I now consider the clients I serve as extended family. My impact on the senior community has filled me with gratitude. I, too, will be a senior one day, and useful information about brain health benefits me and anyone interested in listening just a little while learning a whole lot. *I am honored to passionately share strategies for proactively aging well—mind and body.*

There are so many books about aging. Furthermore, there are tons of publications about brain health. My goal is to create a resource that is not too long-winded or overbearing so folks do not feel intimidated. Instead, I want to create a book that is easy to read and user-friendly. After surveying many adults over fifty years old, results proved that most people give up before trying because how-to material can sometimes take too much time to read and digest. *This book will hopefully provide a get-started-now burst of enthusiasm alongside steady application*. Take your time as you read. Truly digest the information and answer all of the questions that may arise in your mind. Write things down on the notes pages, underline or highlight useful information; let this book work for you.

Yes, as we age, we may move a little slower—we likely need to. We may ache a little more due to stretching less and stressing more. We usually look a little older, because we are! *The reality is that it has taken time and effort to get where we are, but there is still good work to be done each moment we continue to live.*

(Disclaimer: Brain Booster is a research and evidence based program. My advice is second nature to your doctor's orders. Please consult your current health care provider before making any lifestyle changes.)

Part 1

RETIREMENT

It is only fair that people look forward to a legitimate break from working after many years of career commitment or homemaking for their families. However, the myth of waking up late in the day, putting your feet up, and letting life become happenstance has to be broken. Retirement should be qualified, in my opinion. There should be some type of "exitview" with one's physician. How will you spend your days? Is there a cultivating project underway? Are there plans in place for travel? Will you volunteer or work part-time? Will you study or learn a new subject matter? ***Basically, is there a thought-out plan of action, an intent to stay engaged with life?***

As we age, the body and mind need to stay active. Just as physical movement is vital, so is mental stimulation. Slouching on the couch all day will likely lead to aches and pains, bad posture, and weight changes. Similarly, idle minds typically become flabby after retirement. ***These older*** *years, this next chapter, is about reaching down to find the places and things that are still unfinished or even things we never started but wanted to.* Maybe it could be writing that book you've been thinking about, learning that foreign language you find so appealing, or even taking piano lessons.

Don't limit your options; travel can be a wonderful, exploratory undertaking. Venture out for quiet reflection and single-serving decisions that are focused on what you want, strictly for yourself. Many people mistake travel for meaning you have to pack a bag and get on an airplane. Instead, go to local museums and historical sights to make the destination a learning opportunity. Or maybe take a family-and-friends tour, going from city to city or state to state for a given time period to visit folks and learn at least a few new things about the surroundings. While there, stay in and cook delicious meals with fam-friends to create new memories, play board games or cards, go to a local stage play or a live music spot in town, or take a simple after-breakfast or after-dinner walk together. Have meals or just dessert gatherings at great restaurants. Get comfortably dressed up and enjoy new atmospheres and cuisines with those who mean the most to you. Tell stories, yep, get together with family and friends and let everyone tell a life experience of their choice for a few minutes. *These are enjoyable ways to sharpen your mind and have fun too.*

Brain boosting can occur within almost everything we do naturally during a typical day. *The key is to stay consistently involved with life.* Keep in mind that retirement only ends a form of work. Life continues, and we each play a huge part in how we move forward. Some people need to continue working, reducing to a part-time schedule. They need the commitment to stay connected; they need the structured activity. And that's OK.

How you retire is a very unique process. Be honest with yourself. What does retirement look like for you? Are you excited about your next steps? Do you have next steps? Ask yourself the same questions you would need to know in order to marry someone. Seriously, as an exercise, list the top ten to twelve things you'd like to know about your potential life partner before matrimony. Now, answer those questions for yourself—honestly, please. Within those answers are areas to be improved, discovered interests, and life-changing realities about who we are and who we want to become. Don't forget, you're still alive! *Take the time to really live!*

Retirement is the time to tailor-make a productive, goal-oriented schedule, incorporating loads of good times. *Think of all the things you wished you could've done when time didn't allow for much wiggle room.* Did you want to ride your bike or take a walk on weekday mornings? Read for an hour in the backyard while having a late breakfast with coffee and pastries? Maybe just be quiet and meditate for thirty minutes? These are the activities to bake in between all of your must-dos during retirement years. Plan a midweek event with friends, just intended to bring jolly laughter and create new memories. Schedule a coffee or tea walk with a friend to catch up, as opposed to the normal "meet for lunch or happy hour" sit-down scenario. Shake things up a bit, add little touches of pizazz here and there, and you will feel a sprinkle of youth and a new pep in your step.

Keep living, making plans to progress, and working toward your goals. *Keep being more of a better "you" every day.* Continue finding out more about yourself for the rest of your life. Many people are afraid of digging; they're not sure what they'll do with what they find. Self-analysis is a real and mature inquiry. The lack of self-knowledge can show up in a weakened confidence far too often. Stay authentic in your search; open up to explore yourself. We all exist for good reason. Remember, there is only one you, and you deserve to live in your truth. Everyone has something to contribute to this life. Keep your dreams alive by pursuing them steadily, by pursuing yourself heavily. You are worth it!

Thoughts and Notes about Retirement

_____

_____

_____

_____

_____

_____

_____

_____

_____

_____

PURPOSE

Every human desires to be seen and appreciated, perhaps by family, at work, within our households, and even in our communities. We stand out when we feel good about our actions. Self-knowledge allows us to pinpoint our strengths and weaknesses. The more we understand where we are and who we are, the more we can envision where we are going. Armed with that knowledge, each life lesson has the potential to guide. Our talents are revealed on the road to joy. Have reflective moments alone to acknowledge where you are. ***The reality of our current moment often dictates our next moment.***

It is said that the loudest voice of discouragement as we age is our own. I believe that. There can be a sizable amount of self-esteem issues surmounting as we age: gravity takes over, our metabolism slows, the mind drifts more, and vision changes, literally and figuratively. At times we don't recognize parts of ourselves. Well, that whole inside-out concept is alive and kicking. ***What are you all about on the inside?*** How interesting are you? What do you stand for? Are you passionately connected to something you do on a regular basis? Where is your true beauty? What is your true beauty? As we age, principles often matter more, and intrigue can be surprisingly influential for ourselves and others.

Every single person has a specific purpose on this planet. Finding that purpose is what life is all about. ***Take time to be purposed on purpose; search it, feed it, live it.***

Thoughts and Notes about Purpose

_____

_____

_____

_____

_____

_____

_____

_____

_____

_____

_____

LIFEWORK

It is understandable that confidence and knowledge are so closely linked. Any surety brings a feeling of relief. When I can see where I'm stepping, I'm much more comfortable than I am walking aimlessly in the dark. Hence, understanding myself more leads to a more confident me. A big part of who we are is how we spend time earning our living. There are many people who have to do what they have to do and get jobs that are far from their dream job. Oftentimes, they excel and become good, even very successful, at what they do. But there may be a hole, a missing piece or two, something still unfulfilled. One awesome test of finding your purpose and measuring it, so to say, is whether the thought of retirement brings some level of sadness. Does the thought of not doing that thing feel a little threatening to your happiness because you love doing it so much? Lifework is about finding what truly intrigues you, fills you, and represents you well. ***When you unfold what you are here to*** *do, you meet a phenomenal side of yourself.* That should be valued and cared for.

As we get older, we still should stay focused on what needs to get done that is attached to our unique ambitions. If I'm still living in two, five, ten, or maybe twenty-five years, what could I still accomplish? *Our lifework is exactly that—work that takes our lifetime to fully achieve.* Sean Combs said it well: "Can't stop, won't stop!" Now that's a great mantra for living life to the fullest!

Thoughts and Notes about Lifework

_____

_____

_____

_____

_____

_____

_____

_____

_____

_____

Part 2

NEUROPLASTICITY

Simply accepting the concept of neuroplasticity is good for your health! That's powerful. There's mere appreciation for the fact that, if we choose, we can rewire our brains, enabling them to grow new neurons and function at a higher capacity. That's exciting to say the least and exhilarating if I'm a doer. Let's jump right in since *the sooner we start doing something, the closer our desired results are, right?* You may ask, what exactly is neuroplasticity, and why should its practices be incorporated into my daily life?

Neuroplasticity is the brain's ability to grow new neurons. Neurogenesis is the actual growth of new neurons. Neurogenesis is the result of neuroplasticity. *The science behind neuroplasticity proves that new pathways are formed when we learn new information.* Taking on new in-depth studies on a continuous, measurable basis is one of the most beneficial ways to incite neuroplasticity. Maintaining a personal, measurable curriculum can strengthen your brain activity. Think about it. The theory used to be that we were born with a certain capacity of brain cells, and they grew and multiplied for years, until we are about eighteen or maybe twenty years old. Then, throughout our late 40s and into our 50s, cells slowly began to die off. That was just what we thought happened. That was what we thought getting old was. Then we would eventually wither away. Nope! Science now proves that's not what happens.

The hippocampus is a seahorse-shaped organ in the brain. Humans have two hippocampi. They house short-term memories. Unless there is a direct injury to the hippocampi, they can strengthen at any time in our lives. When we receive positive mental stimulation, we invigorate our hippocampi. Like the other parts of our bodies, we have to use them to keep them in shape. The same goes for our brain. We must use it, keep it going, and provide the tools and measures for it to strengthen. Just as it takes time and hard work to acquire and maintain a washboard abdomen, it takes dedication to build and maintain mental agility. Both the brain and hippocampi enjoy effort. They enjoy experiencing repeated determination more than immediate success. The brain wants to be strong all the time, just as we want our entire bodies to be. Be serious about spending time on your brain health every day! Remember that the ego likes instant gratification, but the brain rewards effort. *Consistency breeds success.* It all seems like a lot, but the bottom line is that it's not more tiring to think of all we need to do to be truly healthy than it is disappointing to think of how life could be if we fail before we try.

The return on your mental investment is priceless. Neuroplasticity begs us to eagerly seek new ventures. Furthering our knowledge in a particular topic is not bad for us—it's growth for sure. However, novel information increases the number of "pings." New information pulls any related pieces already in our cerebral file cabinet. Then as information is freshly absorbed, the connections between old and new take place and new pathways light up on our mental map, even when the destination is somewhere we have already been. The benefit is the new route to get there.

Thoughts and Notes about Neuroplasticity

_____

_____

_____

_____

_____

_____

_____

_____

_____

_____

_____

LOGIC

Let's make sense out of some things. As humans, we are figurative guinea pigs more often than we may think. Every time we take a cold pill or try a newly manufactured product, we experiment. What's ironic is that we are much less likely to conduct our own research in natural, more homeopathic ways to be well. We often underestimate the power of our bodies and minds to recalibrate and heal in ways that tap into our innate human abilities. *Taking small, consistent steps toward our bigger health goals is a realistic tactic that will lead to long-term success.*

Logic is the main reason to practice brain care. In the years to come, none of us know what we're headed for—not in regard to health, money, family, or really anything. We can do everything correctly; we can live and eat properly and have clean integrity but still end up with a disease or illness, financial woes, or loneliness. Logically, if any of those things ever arise, it would be nice to be able to say we weren't contributors to them. Of course, we don't set out to hurt ourselves intentionally. However, just as doing a deliberate physical act of harm against ourselves has consequences, avoiding the necessary brain work that can prevent a foggy older life is self-destructive. That's clear-cut logic. *There is no sooner time to start or ramp up your healthy brain habits than now!*

Memory related illnesses have increased tremendously over the past twenty years. Many folks are entering their golden years and being forced to forget everything they've ever known. To be told that, in terms of brain health, we can either stay where we are or get better is great news. The results lie in the work we do right now. No matter where any of us are in life—thirty-five, fifty, seventy years old, or older—we can start right now with the intention to improve our brain health. Yes, we all should strive to be better. In many health arenas, it can often be helpful in the long run to at least not get worse. Health maintenance can be a wonderful stepping stone to progress and healing. Most importantly, *proactive measures can bring tremendous peace of mind because they mean you are taking your mental and physical health seriously.*

Thoughts and Notes about Logic

_____

_____

_____

_____

_____

_____

_____

_____

_____

_____

_____

PRIMED EVERY DAY

There is no time in our lives when we shouldn't be learning. As babies we go from learning how to eat to learning how to talk and walk. Once in school, we learn the ABC's, addition, and subtraction, which segue into learning how to read and write. These skills pivot into detailed research, pragmatic essays, and systematic problem-solving. Some of us attend college or technical schools in early adulthood, aspiring to learn skills to secure our career path. Once our path is found, we actively seek ways to become better at what we do professionally. Business and personal relationships (hopefully) mature and teach us how to negotiate our feelings and demands within the realms of authenticity. Learning is a never-ending task, which benefits every part of our lives, especially our brains and their ability to function properly.

The moment we stop learning, a slow death of sorts begins. Think about it. We are forever changing, so even after forty years of marriage, you'll still have more to learn about the spouse you think you know so well. We change. Our views and opinions change. Business tactics and concepts, social norms and trends, and lots of other things change with each new generation. Technology is growing so fast that many people have to stay ahead of the learning curve to remain relevant and successful. Being adaptable and willing to engage in conversations about new ways of doing things is a grand reason to have a genuine connection with a younger person; a grandchild, a co-worker, a niece or nephew. The world around us will keep changing. The question is, how open to changing will we be as we age?

Similarly, we must continue to dig into ourselves and keep learning how to be better. Many people just lock into who they believe they are on a surface level, never examining their full potential. Human growth is being able to move forward and adapt to the everyday newness of life. ***Every day is a new day for everything.***

Research conducted by the Cleveland Clinic and many other science and health publications shows that there are six basic things that should be incorporated into each day to keep the memory and brain functioning well. I have created an acronym to help remember theses six basics: PRIMED.

At the end of each day, it should take you about thirty seconds to ask yourself, *am I primed? Have I touched on all six components today?* So what is the meaning of PRIMED? The dictionary defines primed as to prepare or make oneself ready for a particular purpose. In the context of this book, **we should ensure that we are PRIMED for our everyday life and the years ahead of us.**

Prime yourself to stay active and open to new ideas, information, and opportunities. *Intentionally care for your brain.* Make it a priority to find realistic approaches in your daily life to stay primed. Take a look at the six categories of PRIMED, and then we will go into detail for each one. The six categories of PRIMED are **P**uzzles, **R**est, **I**nteraction, **M**editation, **E**xercise, and **D**iet.

PUZZLES

Not just crosswords or word searches, but puzzles of all sorts. Challenges may actually be a better word. ***The brain wants and needs to be stimulated.*** New activity is the best stimulation for the brain to flourish!

Whatever responsibilities you had during your thirties, forties, and fifties, they likely kept you busy and always striving for better. Whether you were raising children, keeping a marriage together, getting a promotion or even starting a new job, buying property, starting and keeping a business, balancing a budget, planning for the holidays each year, and so on, those were the "puzzles" that kept your brain busy. The very things you probably complained about and wished to be done with at times were helping your brain. There's this obscure dream, imposed on us by society; one day life will be total leisure, with frequent visits to and from visitors, traveling adventures, shopping sprees, and unlimited resting, all intertwined excitedly into each day. Not! I'm not saying that these things can't be a part of your reality, just not all of every day! *There is still lots to do and much more to accomplish.* There are still plenty of things to figure out. That's what life is all about. Remember, you're still alive!

Finding excitement about staying mentally fit can be a realistic concern. Take time to examine yourself and your history to identify your motivational triggers. No one can do this work for you. Ask yourself, what were some of the ways you stayed pumped about your endeavors when you were younger? What was your reasoning? What "did it" for you then? What "does it" for you now? Is it when you exercise routinely or eat healthier? Maybe it's when your hair is shorter or dyed a certain color. Or maybe it's a particular style of clothing that makes you feel your best. Sometimes it can be a certain setting. Do you tend to stay more disciplined when you study or work at the library? Your favorite coffee shop? At home? *When or how are you at your best?*

Find as many positive triggers as you can and spend time being productive through them. Go study or meet with a book club at the local coffee shop. Get a hairstyle that makes you feel a bit racy. Buy a completely different color or style shirt than you normally wear. Find semi-extreme but complimentary things that enhance your every day. You should like the gym you go to if you're expected to go to the gym, right? Same holds true for your setup to seriously study and learn. ***Find the environments that settle and inspire you.*** It may be your backyard or a nearby park. Go to the library once a week on a certain day. Take a hot latte or smoothie along, and go to learn or to work on a continuous project. Try to take an hour or more to sit quietly and study something seriously. Amplify the benefits by then going to sit at the computer or use a journal and take fifteen to thirty minutes to type or write everything you remember about what you just studied. This is an example of an excellent "puzzle." Plus, you learned something new. There are tons of ways to excite your neurons using various puzzles.

Vocabulary and languages are high on the list of challenging activities that promote brain cell growth. Learning new words and sounds are great, but utilizing them regularly is where the magic happens. To learn a new word, its origin, how to use it in a sentence, a few synonyms and antonyms, and so on is actually wonderful. Making the commitment to use that new word once or twice a day for the next week, and following through, steps everything up a notch. The brain thrives off of making new connections. This causes those positive "pings" we mentioned earlier.

Make a choice to underline words you don't know when you're reading, and then look them up when you have time. Use those new words in conversations and correspondence. Create a word journal if you're a wordsmith, and from time to time, write healthy sentences, short stories, jingles, or poems using your new words. ***Vocabulary is always good brain food at any age.***

Do you have the urge to learn a new language? Do it! Some believe that learning a new language is a sign of great intelligence because of the commitment it takes to do it. There are so many language learning apps and books available. Check with your local library for their online and hard copy learning resources. Use the app store on your smartphone or the search engine on your computer to find user-friendly language teaching platforms. Find self-supporting ways to stay active while studying, like watching a thirty minute soap opera every day or reading a magazine in whatever language you choose to learn. ***Structure your learning and studying time, and show up determined.*** Small steps everyday will lead to the success you desire.

Right under My Nose

A new resident, Anna, moved into one of the facilities where I teach my Brain Booster class. I can recall her first day attending class. Everyone welcomed Anna, and you could easily tell how comfortable that made her feel. I asked her to tell us a few things about herself, and she did modestly. Anna had a beautiful accent that we learned was from growing up in Armenia. After class that day, another resident, Ida, approached Anna and admitted that she always wanted to learn Armenian because she had a friend years ago that was Armenian, but they had lost contact. Ida told Anna the few words she knew in Armenian. I enjoyed hearing the laughter of a new friendship in the making. The two ladies made an agreement to begin sitting together in the dining room for meals. Anna suggested that they only speak Armenian each night at dinner. Anna was patient in her casual teachings, and they both enjoyed the commitment to progress. After several months, Anna was speaking to Ida in Armenian before and after my class and Ida was conversing back, in Armenian! I was overjoyed by their determination and results of these ladies' creativity. Ida gained an indirect connection to her long ago friend, and Anna made a new friend in her new building that kept her connected to her past. They both gave their brains consistent stimulation that strengthened their neurons.

Playing an instrument is another great task for the brain. Music, on many levels, is fertilizer for neuronal growth. Studying under an instructor is ideal, but you can also self-teach. Whether you refer to YouTube or an instructional manual, self-teaching an instrument can be fun and can offer a wonderful sense of accomplishment. Either way, *take your lessons seriously, practice every day.*

Music has a multilayered effect because of the many human components involved. Learning and playing an instrument usually forces its lucky victim to live in the moment. It takes focus, auditory attention, and learned coordination to truly play an instrument correctly. *Simply appreciating music can also improve brain health.* Sitting quietly and focused on a piece of music or studying a favorite artist is useful time spent bettering your cognition.

Here's an interesting approach: choose a musical artist in any genre and pick the same time two to four days a week to listen to their music, learn their backstory, study their lyrics, and dance! (Safely, of course.) *Dancing is the icing on the cake.* When you transfer your feelings and comprehension of the music into movement, major sparks happen! The mind and body feel how free you are.

You can't really dance and be in a bad mood at the same time because dancing makes you vulnerable. Dancing can be a free three- or four-minute (or more) vacation from any stress whenever you choose. Dance when you have a great doctor's visit, or a not so great visit. Dance, in thanks after you eat good food, or any food. Dance when you think of a laughable moment with someone you love. Dance when a tough moment has finally passed. My point is, use dance as a celebratory tool, as a lift-me-up tactic, more often. Rhythmic body motion lightens us up, mind, body, and soul. Dancing is also a form of exercise so use it at home by playing two or three upbeat songs back-to-back and dancing nonstop. Again, stay safe. ***Turn up the volume a bit and get your groove on!***

Day In and Day Out

One of my favorite stories is about a man, Mark, who lives in another retirement home where I teach my Brain Booster class. After listening to my discussion on the favorable impact music has on the brain and memory, Mark decided that he wanted to pursue the harmonica. He admitted his envy of those who were well-versed at the instrument. He told me it was amazing to hear such beautiful sounds from such a small device. So Mark bought a harmonica and began practicing every day in a distant outdoor corner of one of his building's whimsical courtyards. I laughed when he said he chose that spot because he didn't want anyone to complain about the awful noise radiating from his weakened lungs. But Mark stayed consistent. He practiced—a focused practice—at least three to five days a week from 11 a.m. to noon each day. This went on for about five months, with his neighbors making innocent jokes and curious stares. After several more months, Mark noticed that some of his fellow residents were beginning to sit in the lounge chairs spread throughout that same courtyard at right about the same time as his practice. Was it a coincidence? No, they were coming to hear Mark! By then, he had developed a skill set laced with confidence and determination. His daily practice turned into a free and wonderful source of entertainment for Mark and many others. More so, his biggest and definitely most jovial fans were Mark's brain cells.

Vocabulary, languages, and music are just a few "puzzles" that have been proven effective in warding off memory issues as we get older. Keep the wheels of your mind well-oiled with intriguing experiences that continue to feed your intellect. Try to always know (1) your current learning goals and where you are in terms of your continuance or accomplishment and (2) what your next step is going to be. Keep notes and jot down your thoughts as well as your ideas and plans of action. ***You should always keep yourself on a curriculum of some kind.***

There are great puzzle books to keep bedside or couchside. Even toilet-side if that works for you. Try to find mixed puzzle books with some or all of the following criteria:

- Progressive challenges: going from easy to difficult as you advance through the book

- Puzzles marked with the challenged memory function(s) it addresses

- A wide variety of puzzle styles, both numerical and textual formats

Thoughts and Notes about Puzzles

_____

_____

_____

_____

_____

_____

_____

_____

_____

_____

_____

REST

Whenever you go to the doctor, for any reason, one of the most consistent pieces of advice you'll receive is to get proper rest. ***Sleep is the single most utilized behavior experienced by humans.*** However, the decline of the value of sleep over time is mind-blowing. Historically, rest has been a topic that has, at times, gone from heavily valued to heavily shunned.

Check this out! Esteemed poet and playwright William Shakespeare said, "Sleep is the heavy honey dew of slumber; it's nature's soft nurse." While prolific Elizabethan writer Thomas Dekker said, ***"Sleep is the golden chain that ties health and our bodies together."*** However, renowned inventor Thomas Edison said, "Sleep is a chronic waste of time." And the ironclad former Prime Minister of England Margaret Thatcher said, "Sleep is for wimps."

Many people underestimate the damage that results from sleep deprivation. Let's explore what happens when we sleep. While resting, the body recalibrates. Notice how many medications have drowsiness as a side effect. Even medicine works better when you are quiet and still. We humans are machines. ***The way we treat our bodies and minds reflect most directly in our health.*** Our internal components work systematically to deliver life. Some people may need more mental rest than others, while some may be in a position of physical labor at work and need quality physical rest for their aches and pains, and others may stare at a computer screen all day and need ocular rest. All humans have to shut down for a consistent amount of hours each day to reap the long-term benefits of proper sleep.

When we settle our bodies down, it is much easier for our systems to work properly. Think about a car that needs maintenance. The mechanic cannot work on the vehicle while it's moving or the engine is still running. They need the car to be still and stop running. ***Falling into a deep and uninterrupted sleep reaps many rewards.*** Aside from the obvious refreshment that good and proper rest affords us, our insides are provided with respectful downtime to operate at their optimal level.

There is a detox that takes place in our brains while we sleep. All kinds of tidying up, filing and reorganizing, loading and unloading, and other necessary updates occur when the body is resting. This process takes a minimum of four uninterrupted hours each night. Yes, we want longer periods of quality sleep, but four uninterrupted hours is the absolute minimum to begin with if you have insomniac tendencies. Taking measures to find what works for your individual circumstances is a priority, because a true healthy night's sleep is seven to nine uninterrupted hours.

Poor sleep is a main contributor to memory decline and different brain afflictions. When your computer doesn't update its software, it malfunctions and operates slowly. The same with your brain. When sleep-deprived, you may experience a foggy feeling in your head and some of your reactions may be delayed. Normal routines might even seem confusing.

Rest allows your interior battery to recharge. By getting sufficient rest, your brain has been optimized to its healthiest state. ***Something as easy as adequate sleep can add loads of value to your everyday life!***

There are many reasons why people tussle with a good night's sleep. Some have to get up several times to use the bathroom, while others lay awake and overthink things. The rest of this section discusses some tactics that may help you to overcome the menaces that are keeping you from ample slumber.

Water intake is extremely important but can send us to the bathroom often. First, let's talk about why water is so critical. ***Hydration supports positive brain health.*** Water flushes toxins from all of our organs and even acts as a lubricant. Think of water like oil in a car. It runs through our system to wash out impurities. Our kidneys depend on water to function properly. Movement becomes much more comfortable and pain is decreased when we are properly hydrated. When anything is dry, it turns brittle. Brittle things break easily and cannot bend and move with ease. In turn, dehydrated people tend to have more body aches, break bones easier, and have more difficulty moving around.

The Centers for Disease Control and Prevention state that every part of our health is enhanced when we maintain hydration. Water hydrates the spinal cord, brain, and various tissues. Imagine a dry sponge, hard and impermeable. That's how dehydration presents itself in our body. We want well-moistened tissues to absorb the good stuff and heighten elasticity. Our brain should be hydrated as well, to enhance learning and growth in a healthy manner. The brain has so many messages to process all day, every day. Thus, dehydration will surely lead to mental delays. In addition, proper hydration helps with saliva formation. Saliva aids in proper digestion and keeps our eyes, mouth, and nose moist. Our skin is more firm when we stay hydrated. Proper water intake also keeps our mouths cleaner. Less sugar and more water can improve dental hygiene. Last but not least, ingesting sufficient water helps maintain and even lose weight.

Most people don't know how much water they should drink each day. *To calculate the number of ounces you need daily, take your body weight and then divide that number in half.* That's your minimum daily requirement of water. Try to finish that requirement by four or five every evening, especially if you are getting up for nightly bathroom runs. That doesn't mean that you cannot drink anything for the rest of the night. You won't be as thirsty because your body will have its daily requirement so you can take sips here and there purely out of desire. This method allows your bladder to empty two to four times before going to sleep. If you are a night owl, finish your daily water intake approximately two to four hours before your bedtime. The closer it gets to bedtime, limit drinking any kind of liquid to a minimum.

Medications can have frequent urination as a side effect. Talk to your doctor immediately if you think your medication is taking you on bathroom night-runs. Ask if you can either change the time or the frequency you take the medicine so that you are not interrupting your necessary rest while still handling the health concern that the medication addresses. ***Be a respectful advocate for yourself***, especially with the health professionals you interact with. Make sure that you marry their professionalism with your beliefs and instincts. A trustworthy doctor is confident about their recommendations and is able to explore options that take your values along with your needs into consideration.

Caffeine should never be ingested after lunch, especially if you are a restless sleeper. Limiting your daily intake of caffeine can lead to better rest at night. Most of us enjoy some form of caffeine but remember that it depletes your hydration levels! Therefore, a good rule of thumb is to ***use water to earn caffeine***. For instance, make a deal with yourself that an extra bottle of water earns you a small cup of coffee. This has dual benefits: limiting caffeine intake and maintaining hydration.

Relaxers can be very helpful and aid in your sleep quality. Lavender essential oil can produce a calming effect when dabbed behind the ears. For a more relaxed effect, put a dab under your nose. Whenever using essential oils, always use a cotton swab to apply, never your finger. *Lavender in any form can be soothing.* Another great tactic for better slumber is lavender lotion. Massaging a little onto your hands, neck, and arms can send you to dreamland.

Our internal body clock works best when we take measures to reinforce our routines. Ambiance can act as another relaxer. Make sure your bedroom lighting is dimmed at least thirty minutes before bedtime. Invest in a nightlight for your bedroom and bathroom so moving around safely in the night doesn't force you to turn on bright lights. If you typically go to sleep with the television on, set the sleep timer for thirty to sixty minutes. This helps in case you wake up again. The blue light from the screen can affect your ability to fall back to sleep. This holds true for cell phones and computer screens too. Turn computers off each night. If you need to keep your cell phone on, turn the ringer on low and place it face down near you, but preferably not in the bed with you. Likewise, wake your bedroom up when you rise each day. Open the curtains and blinds and make the bed. Try not to use your bed as a place to lie around during the day. Let your bed be for sleeping only.

There are also foods that aid in good rest. Believe it or not, kiwifruits, bananas, and blueberries are tasty treats that will help you sleep better. A small cup of hot caffeine-free tea, especially chamomile tea, or warm milk can relax you from the inside. Almonds and walnuts can help you sleep better too. These foods are not sleep remedies, but they all have properties that can contribute to quality rest. If you must have a late-night snack, try one of the above mentioned options. Avoid heavy foods late at night; they will stimulate your digestive system and cause you to toss and turn.

So what should you do when you unwillingly wake up through the night? Well, what you should not do is lay in your thoughts, especially if they are stressful. *Pondering stressful thoughts is unhealthy for brain cells, especially when said thoughts are negative.* Use the bathroom if that's what woke you up. Shift your sleeping position if necessary. If you are still up fifteen to thirty minutes later, take more soothing action, like meditation or turning on low volume instrumental music or nature sounds. Having a calming meditation app or a classical or jazz music station on your cell phone comes in handy during a sleepless night. Lay still and use a meditation technique to clear your head and settle down into a calmness that can send you back to sleep. Nighty night, I truly hope you sleep tight.

Thoughts and Notes about Rest

_____

_____

_____

_____

_____

_____

_____

_____

_____

_____

INTERACTION

It is very important that we stay social. ***Our brains benefit from being in all types of interactive environments.*** Let's be clear, you don't have to be a social butterfly to receive the advantages of socialization. Even when we stay reserved in our approach, our brains are learning through everything that we experience. When we choose to speak in conversations, our brains react and develop through the questions we ask and the replies we receive and offer. The point is to fully employ your mind in the interaction taking place, in whatever way that works best for you. For example, attending a lecture allows you to learn the information being presented, but you also register the smell of the room. It could be a new smell for you. Or it could be a nostalgic smell that leads your brain to a memory. You also register the various colors and different kinds of people in the room, the layout of the furniture, the paint on the walls, and maybe there's a unique lighting fixture that catches your eye. More times than not, something in that social setting is a teaching moment. Something, or many things, may cause your brain to curiously ask questions and take notes. Likewise, going to breakfast, lunch, or dinner parties allows the sense of taste to silently ask the brain to notice the ingredients, judge whether it likes it or not, and consider its nutritional impact. Whatever the case may be, engagement of all sorts can be mentally beneficial.

Our personal investment while we participate in certain scenarios plays a major part in the benefits they provide us. Choosing to be fully present can be a key factor. How many times do we hurriedly scarf down food, not even chewing it properly for digestion, yet alone appreciation. When attending an event that is personally significant, like a wedding or birthday celebration, make sure to garner the mental perks of human connectivity.

Similarly, one-on-one conversations are often a missed opportunity for great neuronal growth. Many people do not give their undivided attention in their personal interactions. When talking to a friend or family member, in person or on the phone, it's rare that we sit down, turn the television off, and take the time to truly invest in what is being said. Listen to your conversation partner's inflections, which are often truth-tellers, and expressions. *There are*

hidden jewels within dedicated spaces. Many functions of the brain appreciate being able to maximize through focus and attention.

Finding people to laugh with is great synergy. ***There is healing in laughter.*** Everyone should have someone, or a few folks, that, without a doubt, will incite laughter. Also, keep a noted collection of funny movies or shows that you can tune into for a laugh. Don't be fooled, there is surely such a thing as "singular interaction." You can be by yourself and have joyful, constructive moments. Watching a video or listening to a podcast from your favorite comedian can cause positive brain stimulation. Laughter, alone or with others, releases positive endorphins and loosens our insides. The brain included! Everything works better when we lighten up and relax. Laughter is a free dose of adrenaline. Get as much as you can, as often as you can.

You should be concerned if you or someone you know begins to isolate themselves. Human communication and connection is a part of healthy living and aging. We all benefit from having reciprocal relationships. You need not have tons of friends or family that you consistently keep in touch with or hang out with. Quality over quantity is the key. Make sure your social settings leave you feeling positive and encouraged. Stay clear of people or events that are simply time fillers. Typically, if it doesn't feel right, it's not right. Trust your intuition. *The brain benefits most from interactions that put a smile in your heart.*

Thoughts and Notes about Interaction

_____

_____

_____

_____

_____

_____

_____

_____

_____

_____

_____

_____

MEDITATION

Anyone who has attended my Brain Booster class will tell you that I place a star by meditation and declare that meditation is the most important part of staying PRIMED. Why? ***Every single experience in life is mind over matter.*** Despite this being an extremely popular cliché, everyone stops to contemplate this statement once they truly understand it. We all have stressful times. The actuality is that in those moments, the matter is on top of our mind, so we have a tough time navigating through it. Meditation is a practice that allows calmness to become our default setting. At our most difficult crossroads, meditation affords us the ability to act effectively and not let ourselves become infected with negativity or agitation. The turmoil that takes place in our mind when we lose control of our mental compass can lead to much harm, in both our bodies and brains. Another important aspect of meditation is that it is less about the correlation to a particular religious or spiritual belief, rather it's more about finding peace through awareness.

My son has always been an old soul. He has said things to me over the years that have become law in my world. We both experienced tough times when he was very young, and in those moments, meditation turned out to be a powerful tool. He looked at me once during that time, tapping on one side of his head with his pointer finger, and said, "Be careful what you eat." The tears began to well in my eyes as he spoke and I listened. He went on to tell me how the eating we do with our mouth is much more easily digested into waste than the words and images we put in our minds. He is very much correct! ***Meditation is a beautiful sanctuary where we can repeatedly cleanse and refill our mind with healthy "food."*** There are often negative things that we ruminate on in our minds for years. Untruths about who we are or what we cannot have or reach. Sometimes people can say and do mean things that stick with us longer than they should. Let meditation be a still conversation with your soul that reinforces what you know for sure, what you want, and that ever-so-cleansing exhale of all that may need to be released.

A wellness retreat that I attended once gave a beautiful template for meditation. The instructor asked us the following three simple questions:

1. *Who are you?*
2. *What do you want?*
3. *What are you grateful for?*

Brilliant! The answers to these questions will surely change as you grow and change. Inhale—pulling in deeply through the nose, into the belly (big belly), and holding it in for a few seconds—and answer the first question simply. Then exhale slowly—through the mouth or nose, letting all air out of the belly—and release whatever it is that holds you back from your first answer.

I will be vulnerable with you, only to give an example. Inhale. *Who am I? Love.* Hold it, accept it. Exhale. *What holds me back? Hurt.* Kindly release it through a steady breath out. While in meditation, do not address your focus points in detail, just make them known. You can journal afterward if you'd like to go deeper. During the meditation, stay focused on simple answers that allow you to not get caught up in the specifics. Answer the three questions repeatedly for your entire pre-determined time commitment in the manner explained. **Continuously remind yourself of who you are and who you are not.** Powerful affirmation takes place in this space.

There are many forms of meditation. The beauty is that there is an option for everyone. Different meditation forms require different skills and mindsets. ***Explore the practices that encourage you and always remain open to the experience.*** A regular meditation practice can help reduce anxiety, depression, insomnia, general pain, and high blood pressure. The rest of this section explores some of the most commonly utilized forms of meditation.

Mindfulness meditation is most popular in the West but originated from Buddhist teachings. During this practice, you pay attention to your thoughts, hence it's called "mindfulness." Don't qualify or judge your thoughts, just notice them and realize the patterns. It may be helpful to focus on your breath or an object. You can do this meditation with your eyes open or closed. When your eyes are open, it is best to focus on one object. If you become distracted, refocus back to your breath or the object. ***Mindfulness meditation combines focus and awareness.*** This meditation is a good practice to do alone. Journaling afterward is usually beneficial. Make note of the thoughts you experience. Over time, this practice can be highly informative about your subconscious self.

Transcendental Meditation is one of the most popular meditations in the world. It is often referred to as TM. This meditation has been studied in the world of science more than any other forms. Published reports from the Cleveland Clinic to trusted articles in Forbes Magazine have named TM to be highly effective for brain function and stress-induced issues. A trained guide will personalize a mantra for you and teach this meditation technique in an individual setting. ***TM allows partakers to transcend beyond the surface level of awareness.*** People who invest in TM instruction typically maintain a continuous meditation practice.

Guided meditation is led by a trained moderator. It can be done one-on-one, but it typically happens in a group setting. The instructor encourages a train of thought by asking questions and enforcing positivity through motivational words. Guided meditation can sometimes have music in the background. Many guided meditations are themed, such as self-compassion, energy healing, or recharging. This meditation can be emotional since you are often prompted to address various matters unexpectedly. However, ***guided meditation can be very healing*** because a skilled teacher will incorporate both investigation and relief during the session.

Movement meditation forces many people to think of yoga. Any form of motion can be used in this meditation, such as walking, cooking, gardening, or even massage. Movement meditation allows your mind to wander a bit as it puts the focus on the activity. Take special notice of the trees or flowers on a walk, feel every sensation during self- or received massage, tune in to smells as you focus on cooking a special recipe, or enjoy the feeling of your hands in the soil or on the dry leaves while planting or pruning. Those that find it hard to stay still can let the physical side of an activity lead them in this meditation. *The key is to stay engaged in the activity and remove other distractions.*

Sidebar 3: Beneficial Multitasking

Marsha, a client that started with me years ago, made it clear that she was not a fan of meditation and was not open to trying it. Months later, she humbly admitted that meditation had come up several times in conversations with her doctor, friends, and even her children. So, she decided to try movement meditation. Marsha lives alone and typically washes the dishes once a day, around 6:00 or 7:00 each evening. She began turning off the television, putting her cell phone in the other room, and quieting her mind while focusing on the sound and feel of the water in the dish pan and coming from the faucet. The water added such a calming component. Marsh never knew those consistent ten minutes each evening would create a mental break that benefited her brain. She says she feels more in control of how she reacts to people and situations since meditating daily.

Spiritual meditation was initially practiced mainly in eastern religions, but now it's more widespread. It can be similar to praying. **Participants focus on silence and breath-work while connecting on a deeper level with their higher power** (religious or spiritual). While meditating, you can quietly say a prayer or hope repeatedly. Spiritual meditation can be overwhelming at times, as you are often leveled to your most basic self. It is common to feel very loving and accepting of who you are after this practice. Essential oils, such as frankincense, myrrh, sage, vetiver, and sandalwood are often used during spiritual meditation. This meditation can be done at places of worship or at home.

Mantra meditation is a part of many different forms of mediation. **Repetitive sounds are used to clear the mind.** The spoken or chanted sound, word, or phrase becomes the focal point. The mantra can be recited quietly or loudly, alone or in a group. Repeating the same mantra causes heightened awareness. People that have a hard time focusing on their breath or that don't like silence usually enjoy mantra meditation.

Focused meditation concentrates on any of the five senses. For example, concentrate on sight by staring at the movement of a candle flame. Concentrate on smell by burning an essential oil and appreciating all the attributes you recognize. Concentrate on hearing by focusing on one instrument in a nonverbal jazz or classical piece. Concentrate on touch by meditating with a rosary or mala beads along with repetitive prayers or chants. Concentrate on taste by reminiscing about a food or beverage that is healthy and self-satisfying. Relax and try to focus on the qualities of the influence. *Find balance in your stillness that links the strength of the influence to yourself.* This meditation is helpful for those who need more focus, but it can be challenging for beginners. Participators usually have to be consistent to find the benefits of focused meditation.

There are even more styles of meditation than those listed here. You may even think of ways to meditate that no one else has. *Meditation is about making a time commitment to settle your mind and find stillness, despite your challenges.* American Buddhist Pema Chodron said, "Meditation is a commitment to stay." No matter how distracted you may become, keep returning to the focus, continue breathing, and don't give up. The willpower and positivity we gain by consistently meditating can come in handy when we need to muscle through a tough time. Making your daily meditation practice congenial and centered will eventually allow your default setting in life to be rational with effective outcomes. Let meditation teach you. In the quietness of our mind, there is much to learn about ourselves.

A healthy brain needs all stressors to be in check. ***The most difficult part of meditation is showing up***. And showing up is really all you need to do. Author and spiritual teacher, Eckhart Tolle, kindly reminds us, "Meditation is being, truly not doing."

Thoughts and Notes about Meditation

_____

_____

_____

_____

_____

_____

_____

_____

_____

_____

_____

EXERCISE

Exercise has more benefits than just keeping you looking good. ***The brain loves the endorphins released during exercise.*** The immune system is heightened when we exercise because our stress hormones are reduced. There are respected theories that believe exercise flushes toxins from the lungs and can also cause antibodies to circulate through white blood cells quicker. Also, infections are better fought when our body temperature rises. Sweating, it turns out, is a healthy measure to calm depression and slow age-related memory loss. Breaking a sweat from exercise also improves sleep, boosts energy, and improves mood.

You will be glad to know that you do not have to enter a half-marathon, jog the block every day, or pump iron in the gym. I teach my clients to do their normal daily exercises safely, and if possible, do it until they start to feel trickles of sweat. We all sweat differently. During workouts, some begin to perspire from their foreheads, while others feel it down the middle of their backs first. Many experience underarm sweat. Regardless, let the sweat drip! *Take pride in the benefits your brain reaps from daily exercise and sweating*.

Even if you are not feeling your best, you can still move some part of your body intentionally every day. *Damage from becoming sedentary happens quicker than most realize.* Making movement a part of your daily routine ensures that you use it and not lose it! Let's look at real scenarios. Say you are in bed with a cold, feeling low on energy. You can do focused leg raises or even ankle rotations while in bed. Perform two 15-minute sessions to concentrate on your form. Use resistance to maximize the effort you are putting forth. Every now and then many people experience constipation or diarrhea. Laying on your back on your bed and pulling your knees toward your rib cage is an effective way to stimulate your system when constipated. Take deep breaths so you can also quiet your mind to make this an exercise/meditation combo. When lowering your legs back down, try to hold them slightly raised to give your core a workout. You can do one leg at a time or both together. If your digestive issues are the opposite that day and you can't stay off the toilet, relax, take deep breaths while you're sitting, then grab a lotion or shampoo bottle and do some arm curls or raises. Alternating your focus to exercising lightly while sitting on the commode usually calms your digestive system. Watching your favorite television shows can be a great exercise time too. Using commercials as a time to exercise provides about fifteen minutes total exercise for a one-hour show. Or use the show time to exercise and the commercials to rest, especially if you have a treadmill or stationary bike at home. By the end of the program, you will have put time in toward your daily goal. Do leg lifts, Kegel exercises, neck stretches, and fist flexor exercises to add variety to the day. The objective is to alert the brain that it can expect consistency.

Find creative ways to incorporate exercise into your daily activities. Most of the things we need to do in life can be done in ways that fit our personalities if we use trial and error to see what is effective and inviting at the same time. The rule of thumb is that by 6:00 p.m., if you have not done your daily thirty minutes of exercise, stop and do it then. *Move every day, no days off!* Walking to the elevator or kitchen does not count as exercise even though the steps are helpful. Remember, exercise is focused and intentional. As we age, exercise and movement have to become daily activities. Don't let your mind or your age tell you differently.

American athlete, Jackie Joyner-Kersee, once said, "Age is no barrier. It's a limitation you put on your mind." If there's one thing it's okay to forget in order to stay motivated, it's your age. Keep moving!

Thoughts and Notes about Exercise

DIET

yes, Yes, YES! You are what you eat! ***Everything we eat feeds our bodies and brains.*** Eating responsibly is a proactive measure to prevent or improve health issues. A balanced diet is the key to many hopeful outcomes. Make sure to get your bloodwork done at least annually so that you know of any vitamin or mineral deficiencies you may have. We can easily get in the habit of thinking everything has to do with age-related decline. However, lacking certain nutrients can often disguise a bigger problem. A vitamin B_{12} or D_3 deficiency is very common. If left untreated, it can cause a person to feel foggy with low energy and mood swings. There are studies that suggest long-term D_3 deficiencies are linked to Alzheimer's disease and certain dementias. Taking vitamins without doctor supervision is not recommended because you may be getting some of what you need from your meals. Knowing what needs to be supplemented prevents chemical imbalances. Keep in mind that having too much of certain nutrients can also pose a threat. Talk to your doctor and have them go over your bloodwork results with you. Then agree on what vitamins or eating habits could help fulfill your needs.

Look up foods that contain the vitamins and minerals you lack. You may be surprised to find delicious options that give you exactly what you need. When you eat, look at your plate and ask, *what will this make me look like and what will this make me feel like?* Of course, we all get weak sometimes. To remedy this truth, I've always said that if you do things right most of the time, you won't feel so bad if you mess up some of the time. Diets that include fresh fruits and vegetables, unprocessed grains, fish, and quality meat choices tend to have the best brain benefits. A doctor I worked with once explained how meat and fish are digested in our systems. As it turns out, beef and pork take six to seven days to digest, poultry takes three to four days, and fresh fish and other seafood take one to two days. So in an ideal world, eating a steak or pork chops once every seven to ten days, or chicken once a week, and considering fish and seafood as a more frequent choice gives our bodies the chance to properly digest the foods that can clog our arteries over time. ***Moderation is a great mantra for most things in life, including our diet.***

Omega-3 and omega-6 fatty acids are extremely import-ant for brain health. Sardines are such an excellent source of these required fatty acids. Salmon and other fish also ward off memory loss and depression. ***Fish oils have anti-in-flammatory properties that benefit our entire bodies.*** Nuts and seeds, such as walnuts, almonds, flaxseeds, and chia seeds provide another form of omega acid that has a milder but still very helpful effect on the body.

Be very mindful of your sugar intake. Most people are unaware that refined sugar feeds cancer. ***Many diseases are nourished by sugar.*** Heart disease, diabetes, high blood pressure, inflammation, depression, and premature aging are all negative impacts of high-sugar diets. Sodas and sweet treats are the top contenders that damage healthy aging. Anything with high-fructose corn syrup should be elim-inated or cut back drastically. Watch your fruit intake as well. Certainly, fruit offers a much healthier form of sugar, but it's still sugar. Try to replace cake and cookie-like des-serts with fresh fruit, homemade popsicles, or unsweetened applesauce sprinkled with nutmeg or cinnamon. Get cre-ative to make better choices and, before long, your palate will change and you will stop craving the things that are bad for you.

Vegetables, especially raw, are great for our bodies and brains. ***Raw vegetables are coarse and help sweep plaque off the colon walls as they are digested.*** Having a nice salad with lunch or dinner is a healthy habit to create. Whenever you eat vegetables, raw or cooked, try to use fresh vegetables. When possible, buy more fresh vegetables than you normally would, wash and dry them well, and then freeze them in portion-sized freezer bags. Since we are on the topic of freezers, freeze fruits and vegetables that are about to go bad and then use them later to cook with or to make smoothies. I can never eat a whole watermelon, so I cut a portion into chunks and freeze them. When I want a refreshing treat, I blend the watermelon chucks with either orange or apple juice. Yummy! When cooking, try to not overcook vegetables because it depletes a lot of the nutrients and also reduces the sweeping power they have as they pass through the colon.

Always follow your doctor's orders when it comes to your diet. Many medications have dietary restrictions. Even in my classes, I am very careful about my dietary suggestions. What's good for one person may be harmful for another. Once you have a clear understanding of the foods that support a healthy lifestyle for your profile, get creative and enjoy eating foods that not only taste good but also make you feel great. We all have to eat and our body should benefit from our choices.

Thoughts and Notes about Diet

_____

_____

_____

_____

_____

_____

_____

_____

_____

_____

Part 3

CLOSING REMARKS

Every stage of our life should include measures that are deliberately intended to strengthen our physical and mental capabilities. My hope is that brain health gets more attention and care before people start to show signs of decline. After all, ***the brain is our most valued organ.*** We need our brain to effectively navigate through life's peaks and valleys for our entire existence.

The power of stillness is extremely healing. Meditation is a practice that you want to know well before you may need it. ***Make meditation a daily habit.*** It can be lifesaving, especially when all other options seem exhausted. Every component of PRIMED is necessary to cultivate optimal brain health. Nevertheless, if the mind is not settled, the PRIMED directives will not truly be effective. Allow your brain to take a break and purge every day. Meditation is a great way to do that.

Science has given great hope to replenishing and rejuvenating neurons through neuroplasticity. Get excited about that! Take serious steps to include brain fitness and wellness in your everyday life. Stay PRIMED! ***There should be intentional evidence that you care about your brain.*** Stop often and ask yourself, *how do I treat my brain?* Then listen to the honest answer your brain gives you.

I am truly grateful for your time and your mind!

ABOUT THE AUTHOR

 Kimberly Mitchell is an educator, memory consultant, and creator of the Brain Booster class. She has spent more than a decade researching various lifestyles and deliberate actions proven to aid in the aging process, particularly impacting the brain and memory. Kimberly enthusiastically teaches individuals and groups, on a mission to dwindle the staggering statistics surrounding Alzheimer's and dementia. Don't Forget, You're Still Alive is her first book.

For more information visit Brainboosterclass.com

Printed in the United States
by Baker & Taylor Publisher Services